# The Pioneer Eagles: Their Story

As Observed and Written
by
Mary Haavisto

Illustrations by Zak Jackson

Copyright © 2022 by Mary Haavisto

All rights reserved. No part of this book may be reproduced or transmitted in any form or by any means, electronic or mechanical, including photocopying, recording, or by any information storage and retrieval system, except in the case of brief quotations embodied in critical articles and reviews, without prior written permission of the publisher.

Printed in the United States of America

*Dedicated to Doris Bremner Erickson,
who imparted her love for birds
to many others, including me.*

# Acknowledgments

*A* sincere thank you to the following people who inspired and encouraged the creation of this work.

Michael Nehila, who introduced me to the Pioneer eagles.

David & Nickie Robbs, who were patient with me and supported their daughter Nina, who created the first illustrations that helped me visualize this book.

Helen Graham, who encouraged me with a "go for it" and guided each step along the way.

Zak Jackson, who brings the eagles to life with his artistic anointing.

Kristine Erickson, who researched self-publishing and provided invaluable editing assistance.

# Contents

The Pioneer Eagles: Their Story     1

*A season of watching Mama and Papa Eagle in the Pacific Northwest*

Repairing The Nest     5
Laying And Hatching The Eggs     7
Mama Eagle To The Rescue     11
A Salmon For The Family     15
A Crowded Nest     17
Branching     19
Learning To Fly     21
The Art Of Landing     23
The Empty Nest     25
On Their Own     27

*Challenges In Subsequent Seasons*

A Warning From Mama Eagle     31
A Big Windstorm     35
Building Again     37

# The Pioneer Eagles: Their Story

About 35 miles south of Seattle, Washington, is a beautiful, fertile valley, with the city of Puyallup lying in the midst of it. On the west side of Puyallup, along busy Pioneer Way, is a tall, old cottonwood tree with a large bald eagle nest in the upper branches. This nest has been used by the same pair of eagles for more than 15 years. The location of the nest is very odd, because a railroad track is right beneath the tree. Trains run along the track several times a day, which never seems to bother the eagles. They go about their lives as though the tracks were not there.

# A SEASON OF WATCHING MAMA AND PAPA EAGLE IN THE PACIFIC NORTHWEST

# Repairing The Nest

As they return to their nest from vacationing in the Puget Sound area for the summer and fall, a new season of the eagles' lives is about to begin. It is the first of February, and Mama and Papa Eagle are ready to repair their nest, which was badly damaged by last year's chicks as they learned how to fly.

The repair work begins. Mama Eagle, who stands about 36 inches tall and has a wingspan of 6 to 7 feet, starts by cleaning out all of last year's debris. Soon, Papa Eagle, who stands about 30 inches tall and has a 6-foot wingspan, comes flying in with a large stick in his talons. He carefully places the stick in the side of the nest, moving it with his beak. When he is satisfied with its placement, he flies off to get another.

Mama Eagle looks at the stick, shakes her head, and then moves it with her beak to where SHE wants it to be. No question who rules this roost. The eagles continue working on the nest until every new stick is in place. Then they cover the sticks with a nice, soft bed of grass and moss, which they gather from nearby fields and trees. The nest is now ready to house the eggs that will soon be laid.

# Laying And Hatching The Eggs

During the month of February, while they built their nest, the eagles had mated. By March 1, the first egg was laid in the nest. The next day, a second egg was laid. For the first few days, Mama Eagle sat on the eggs to keep them warm, periodically turning the eggs with her beak to keep them warm on all sides. During this time, Papa Eagle was busy hunting and fishing and bringing food to Mama Eagle at the nest. Being trimmer and faster, Papa Eagle was the better hunter, although Mama Eagle was no slouch.

After the first few days, Papa Eagle also took his turn sitting on the eggs, freeing Mama Eagle to hunt for herself. The eagles were very diligent to keep the eggs warm, never leaving the nest alone. Through wind and rain, storms, and even occasional snow and sleet, the eagles took turns sitting on the eggs for over 30 days.

Then, on April 6, Mama Eagle felt movement in one of the eggs and she excitedly got up to see what was happening. From his perch in a nearby tree, Papa Eagle saw Mama Eagle's excitement and flew to the nest. One of the chicks had pecked a hole in the egg shell and was struggling to get free. As soon as Papa Eagle saw this, he immediately left the nest. About half an hour later, he came back with a 14-inch trout.

• *Laying And Hatching The Eggs* •

By this time, the chick was completely out of the shell. Mama Eagle began tearing off small pieces of fish and feeding them to the chick. After the chick was fed, Mama Eagle carefully tucked it and the remaining egg under her wings to keep them warm.

The next day the second chick began to peck its way out of the shell, and again the adult eagles watched. Then Papa Eagle flew off and soon came back with another trout. Mama Eagle first fed the new little chick and then the chick that had hatched the day before. Well fed, the chicks settled themselves under Mama's wings to take a nap. For the first few days, the chicks were fed every two or three hours and grew rapidly.

# Mama Eagle
# To The Rescue

It is now May 1, and the chicks have grown enough feathers to stay warm and dry. Though it is no longer necessary for the adult eagles to sit with the chicks in the nest, one adult is always in a nearby tree, watching over them.

One day a red-tailed hawk began circling high above the nest. But with each circle, it got lower and closer. All of a sudden, Mama Eagle, with her wings tucked, came diving out of a nearby tree right at the hawk. Terrorized, the hawk took off and darted around trees and branches and wires and telephone poles trying to lose Mama Eagle, but she stayed right on the hawk's tail. The chicks watched this flying display in wonder. Finally, the hawk flew far enough away that the eagle gave up the chase and returned to the nest to make sure the chicks were okay. That was enough excitement for one day!

• *Mama Eagle To The Rescue* •

As the chicks continued to grow, their appetites became voracious. It took both adults hunting full time to keep them fed. And now, though fish was the preferred diet, every kind of food was brought to the nest. Look out below! Rabbits, chickens, cats, small dogs, ducks, and crows were all targets of the eagles.

Not far from the eagles' nest was a blue heron rookery with about 30 nests. The blue herons were raising chicks at the same time, but the herons were terrified of the eagles. If the eagles flew close to the rookery, all the adult herons would take off from their nests and circle the rookery like a cloud. Occasionally, the eagles would swoop in and steal a heron chick and take it to their own nest. The herons had good reason to be frightened. Although they were larger than the eagles, the herons could not compete with the eagles' beaks and talons.

# A Salmon
# For The Family

One morning Papa Eagle was spotted flying to the nest with a 4 or 5 pound salmon in his talons. This is about the most weight an eagle can carry. Being too exhausted to gain the height of the nest, he had to land on a branch about halfway up the tree. After resting for twenty minutes, Papa

*• The Pioneer Eagles: Their Story •*

Eagle launched out with the salmon and circled the tree several times and finally made it to the nest. This salmon was large enough to feed the entire family for two or three days.

# A Crowded Nest

As the weeks went by and the chicks continued to develop, they now began to look more like eagles instead of balls of grey, fluffy down. The chicks were black in color with yellow beaks and talons. They would not get their white heads and tails until they reached maturity at the age of four or five. The wings of the chicks were also growing, reaching five to six feet in length and stretching from one side of the nest to the other. At times, the nest was beginning to feel a bit crowded.

• *The Pioneer Eagles: Their Story* •

As May turned into June, the chicks spent more and more time spreading their wings and beginning the flying motion of beating their wings. This action strengthened the wing muscles in preparation for the first flights. Eventually, the chicks would beat their wings so fast that the action would lift their bodies one or two feet above the nest.

# Branching

Next, the chicks began to "branch." They would either hop or climb to a branch close by the nest and sit on it, thus strengthening their talons. Soon, it was no problem to flap their way to a branch and then later fly back to the nest. They were getting quite good at managing those long wings.

One morning, one of the chicks moved to the edge of the nest and tried to fly to a branch right below it. Oops!

*• The Pioneer Eagles: Their Story •*

Missed! Down tumbled the chick until it caught itself on a branch about a third of the way down the tree. The chick was shaken up and needed a few minutes to recover. At last, the chick started looking around and then hopped and climbed its way to a different branch above its head - then to another, and then to another. Finally there were no more branches between the chick and the nest.

The particular branch to which the chick had climbed extended out and beyond the edge of the nest. The chick made its way to the end of the branch but there was still a gap of five feet to the edge of the nest. That five feet looked like a mile. The chick sat there for a long time, but finally mustered the courage to launch out and, with a great deal of exertion, flapped his way to the nest and landed rather unceremoniously. He was exhausted and spent the rest of the day lying in the nest.

# LEARNING TO FLY

It is the last week of June and the adult eagles spend very little time in the nest. Since the beaks of the chicks are strong enough to tear their own food, all the adults have to do is drop food in the nest and let the chicks feed themselves. About a week later, Mama and Papa Eagle decide that it is time for the chicks to take their first flight. They stop feeding the chicks,

*The Pioneer Eagles: Their Story*

only dropping food off occasionally in the nest. The chicks begin to slim down and get lighter. Always hungry, the chicks cry out to their parents and beg for food.

# The Art Of Landing

Late one afternoon, Mama Eagle landed in a tree about 150 feet behind the nest tree with a fish in her talons. Mama Eagle began feeding on the fish; one of the chicks, now called a fledgling, was so desperately hungry that it took off from the nest and flew to the back tree and landed awkwardly on a branch above Mama Eagle. This landing business is not so easy.

*The Pioneer Eagles: Their Story*

So proud of her fledgling was Mama Eagle that she flew to the branch on which the chick was sitting and rewarded him with the fish. That fish was gulped down in about four bites. The next day both chicks were seen in the nest; so sometime during the night or early morning, the first fledgling had flown back to the nest.

# The Empty Nest

A couple of days later, the second chick took its first flight. Each day the fledglings flew more often and farther from the nest, still returning periodically to see whether Mama and Papa Eagle had dropped a fish or two in the nest. Also, the fledglings would lie down in the nest and take a break from flying.

• *The Pioneer Eagles: Their Story* •

Then came the day that the eagles were seen one last time for that summer. All four eagles were soaring high above the nesting tree, circling round and round and round. Then they flew off and disappeared. It is assumed that the fledglings, now called juveniles, followed Mama and Papa Eagle back to the Puget Sound, where fish are in abundance for the summer.

# On Their Own

The juveniles learn to fish and hunt from the adult eagles, following them around and even stealing food from their parents or from other eagles. Those that do not learn to hunt for themselves do not survive. The first fall and winter are very difficult for the juveniles. Eagle experts say that only 50% of juveniles survive the first year. Maybe the percentage is a little higher for our eagles since the climate is mild and food is fairly abundant even in winter. The fall coho salmon and the December chum salmon runs greatly help our young

*The Pioneer Eagles: Their Story*

juveniles to survive. After the salmon have spawned, they die and their carcasses litter many streams and rivers throughout the northwest, thus providing much food for the eagles and for a variety of other birds and animals.

# CHALLENGES IN SUBSEQUENT SEASONS

# A Warning
# From Mama Eagle

Another year goes by, and Mama and Papa Eagle successfully hatch and raise one chick, but life is not always fair for the two eagles. The next February arrives and the two adults are busy repairing the nest, laying eggs, and sitting on them the customary 36 days until the eggs hatch. When the

• *The Pioneer Eagles: Their Story* •

chicks are about 10 days old and Mama Eagle is sitting with them in the nest, a strange adult male eagle lands in a branch above the nest and begins to chirp at Mama Eagle. Mama Eagle chirped back at him, warning him to leave. But this was a young male who did not have a mate, and his intention was to steal Mama Eagle and the nest from Papa Eagle.

Suddenly Papa Eagle returns from a hunting trip and lands in the nest, where he chirps a warning to the young eagle. Responding to the warning, the stranger dives into the nest and begins to attack Papa Eagle.

As the three eagles thrash about in the nest, Mama Eagle is pushed over the side and falls almost to the ground. She is caught in some brush and flails about until she is able to right herself. Stunned but not badly injured, she just sits there for

• *A Warning From Mama Eagle* •

many hours. Meanwhile, the young male is no match for the experienced Papa Eagle. He is overcome and chased out of the area. Sadly, the chicks have been crushed during the fighting. They were too small and fragile to survive the weight of three eagles thrashing about in the nest. Early the next morning, Mama and Papa Eagle clean the nest and then fly away. It is too late in the season to lay more eggs and begin again.

# A Big Windstorm

The next year also brings challenges to Mama and Papa Eagle. It is a new season and the two eagles are going about their business repairing and building up the nest. One night in early February, a huge storm rolls into the valley with wind gusts of 60 miles per hour. The old nesting tree is blown down in the storm. It lies on the ground next to the railroad tracks, nest and all. Astounded, the two adults fly round and round where the nest should have been, and there is nothing but empty space.

# Building Again

Not to be defeated, the two eagles begin to build a brand new nest in a large tree about 150 feet behind where the original nest had been. When the nest was half finished, another storm came through the valley and blew down the new nesting tree. Now this is getting frustrating. However, undaunted, the eagles begin again. This time they choose a large cottonwood that stands next to Pioneer Way. They successfully build a new nest and raise their chicks, though they are a couple of weeks late getting started. This season the chicks fledge in the middle of July instead of their usual July 4.

• *The Pioneer Eagles: Their Story* •

*This ends our story about Mama and Papa Eagle. But since eagles can live to the age of 30, their story continues. To this day, the nesting tree still stands next to Pioneer Way, and the eagles—being ever true to their calling—faithfully raise their chicks every season.*

Made in the USA
Monee, IL
06 May 2022